Scotland 1290-97

The great Scottish poet, Robert Burns, mentioned in 1787 that one of the first books he read was *The History of Sir William Wallace*. This book poured into his heart such an ardent love for Scotland, that he said that this love would 'boil along till the flood-gates of life shut in eternal rest'. Now to understand why Burns and the Scots in general so appreciate Wallace's outstanding achievements, it is necessary to describe what took place in the Scotland of Wallace's birth, boyhood and early manhood.

William Wallace, born about 1267 a mile or so from Paisley in Renfrewshire, was the second son of Sir Malcolm Wallace, Laird of Elderslie. Young William worshipped in the stately Benedictine Abbey at Paisley and perhaps received part of his education there. A priest uncle in Dunipace near Dundee also helped in his education. From his freedom-loving family and this uncle he would learn about the ancient freedom and independence of Scotland, soon to be threatened by the events of 1290 and the following years.

In 1290, Queen Margaret, the 'Maid of Norway' died, the last direct descendant of King Alexander III (1249–86), himself the last male direct descendant of the Kings of Scots, for so Scottish kings were designated. Several claimants put themselves forward as entitled to be the new King of Scots. To avoid civil war, they and others asked King Edward I (1272–1307) to arbitrate. The king declared his right to be Overlord of Scotland, based on false premises. Sad to say, the claimants swore fealty to him as 'Sovereign Lord of Scotland' and gave him possession of the royal castles. But Edward did not obtain an unequivocal acknowledgement of his claim to be Overlord from the whole 'community of the realm', i.e. the king's free subjects, who, with him, represented Scotland as a political entity. They replied to Edward that they had no power to reply to his demand in the absence of the King of Scots, to whom such a demand should be addressed and who could reply to it. This was a polite reminder to Edward that only a lawful king acting with the advice of his lieges could answer Edward's claim. He rejected this reply, his first discreditable act in his dealings with independent Scotland.

In 1291 a Court of Claims was set up, twenty-four from Edward's Council, forty each nominated by John Baliol and Robert the Bruce, grandfather of Robert the Bruce, later King of Scots. Next year the Court declared John Baliol to be king, and he, when crowned as King John, swore allegiance to Edward. As Overlord, Edward claimed and exercised the right to hear appeals from Scots against their king's judgements. This angered many in Scotland and things progressed from bad to worse.

In 1294 Edward, being at war with France, summoned King John and some Scots earls and barons to do military service overseas. This was unprecedented and increased the growing resentment to the English overlordship. A revolt of the Welsh against Edward showed the Scots what they too could do. The next year the Scots made an offensive and defensive treaty with France, and consequently war with England. In 1296 Edward returned to England, invaded Scotland, sacked the then Scottish town of Berwick and beat the Scots at Dunbar. This ended the organised fighting, and King John resigned to Edward, who received homage from about 2,000 landowners in Scotland. Significantly neither his brother nor Wallace himself are named in the document containing the names. Already in 1291 their father had refused to swear fealty to Edward and he was later killed in an encounter with the English. Edward appointed his treasurer, Cressingham, administrator of the country.

The Wallace Yew at Elderslie, near Paisley – said to have been planted by Wallace

Heroic Wallace and Bruce

by J. A. Carruth

Jarrold Publishing, Norwich

North Berwick, a little farther up the coast from Dunbar

Paisley Abbey, where the young Wallace once worshipped

Wallace the Liberator 1297-1305

By this time Wallace had performed some deeds of daring against the English and he soon became leader of risings in 1297 against them in different parts of Scotland. Wallace slew the English Sheriff of Lanark and recruits flocked to him, for 'he was a man of outstanding daring and endurance, handsome and very generous'. Evidence shows Wallace fighting as fairly as he could – no indiscriminate slaughter; no imprisonment of women, such as King Edward had done; and protection of churches and clergy – even in England when fighting there. This same year at Hexham Priory, Northumberland, England, he ordered some of his followers who had committed sacrilege to be hanged. Then he asked for Mass to be celebrated, for, like Bruce, he was a man of deep religious faith. He gave the place a letter of protection, no mean achievement to help those in enemy territory.

Wallace was utterly fearless and ruled by an outstanding singleness of purpose – to free Scotland from English domination. Even his enemies never charged him with setting up a personal dictatorship. Charters of Wallace show how careful he was to justify his actions in the name of the king and the community of the realm. He is pre-eminent in that extraordinary assembly of outstanding men and women who grace and ennoble Scotland and indeed the world. He can be said to take pride of place among Calgacus, who resisted the Roman invaders in AD 64; Robert the Bruce, who shattered England's disgraceful designs at Bannockburn in 1314; Mary, Queen of Scots, outstanding advocate of religious freedom and heroic courage in adversity who died unjustly in 1587; Duns Scotus, world-famous theologian; the Marquis of Montrose, who also faced unjust death with intrepid courage in 1650; Flora MacDonald, resourceful saviour of Bonnie Prince Charlie from certain death in 1746; Robert Burns, 1759–96, 'Immortal Memory' for one only thirty-seven at death; David Livingstone, 1813–73, missionary and world-famous explorer; Sir Walter Scott, 1771–1832, patriot and pre-eminent in prose and poetry, and many others.

Soon Wallace controlled much of Scotland. An English force was wrecked and routed at Stirling Bridge, 11 September 1297, and many Scots had high hopes of victory and freedom. Wallace and his co-ruler wrote to Lübeck and Hamburg saying that trade, especially in Scots wool – much sought after then as now, could be resumed 'because the Kingdom of Scotland, thanks be to God, has been recovered by war from the power of the English'.

Hexham Priory, Northumberland

Stirling's historic old bridge

Next year, 1298, Wallace was knighted, a high and well-deserved honour, and elected Guardian, i.e. Governor of Scotland. The Scots' victory at Stirling made Edward hasten from France and invade Scotland with a very large and powerful army. He defeated the Scots at Falkirk, and yet their resistance went on, but about 1304 most surrendered. Scotland was once more English occupied territory.

Wallace had not been idle since Falkirk and kept up the fight. He seems to have gone to France, to the Pope and King Haakon of Norway to obtain help. Now the hunt for Wallace was intensified and he was finally captured at Robroyston near Glasgow on 3 August 1305. Taken to London he was there tried for treason on 23 August. To the charge of treason, Wallace replied: 'I cannot be a traitor, since I never swore fealty to the English king'. All useless. He was hanged, cut down while still alive, disembowelled, mutilated and that magnanimous heart still beating for Scotland and freedom was cast into the fire. All this shows Edward as a small-minded and mean man compared with Wallace. For seven years, 1298–1305, he fought and worked for

Scotland's freedom with supreme constancy, sincerity and tenacity remarkable in any age. His life, crowned by his heroic death, roused Scots to a deeper and stronger sense of unity and freedom.

Patriots are usually honoured by their country in some way. The Scottish tribute to Wallace ranks among the most distinguished. This is the Wallace Monument near where he directed his great triumph of Stirling Bridge, 1297. Here in this noble edifice there is a bronze statue of the hero in chain mail holding aloft his huge sword. Nearby is what is traditionally his famous sword, which in battle 'made great room about him'. The Hall of Arms and the Hall of Heroes also honour our intrepid and fearless patriot. For Scots, the Wallace Monument is a constant inspiration for us to give of our best, as he gave, to help on the weal and welfare of our native land, as he aye counsels us to do by his heroic life and glorious death. His family motto, 'Esperance', i.e. hope, is most appropriate, because his inspiration and leadership made Scots hope and strive for Scotland's freedom, won for ever within ten years at the battle of Bannockburn, 1314.

𝔚allace the 𝔅rave

Great in stature, great in name,
Great in honour, great in fame,
Fearless hero fighting for hame, [home]
Warrior Wallace the Brave.

Great in battle, great in affliction,
Great in others' dereliction,
Greatest in glorious death's infliction,
Immortal Wallace the Brave.

Great in Scottish hearts and minds,
His immortal memory us Scots all binds,
An echo in others' hearts he finds,
Scotland's Wallace the Brave.

Freedom's torch seemed fallen and out.
Of that King Edward hadn't a doubt.
'It flames afresh' was Bruce's shout,
'With me and martyred Wallace the Brave'.

Edward's son and host return,
Exulting they'll triumph at Bannockburn.
There Wallace's triumph through Bruce is won,
God-saved Scots gladdens His midsummer sun.

Heroes you both have wrought as one,
With hearts held high in courage,
Martyred is one, both of you won,
Inspire us now in our age.

24 June 1984. 670th anniversary of the Battle of Bannockburn

On the monument to Wallace's memory at Elderslie, his birthplace, one reads in his own language the words: *Bas agus Buaid* – Death and Victory. Then is added in English: 'His example, devotion and heroism inspired those who came after him to win victory from defeat. His memory remains for all time a source of pride, honour and inspiration to his countrymen'. Then in Latin, the language of his gallant clerical collaborators, is added: 'I tell you the the truth. Freedom is what is best. Son, never live a life like a slave'.

Lord Roseberry, 1847–1929, Scots patriot, British Prime Minister and historian, sums up Wallace's achievement as follows: 'Without him the Scots might never have rallied for defence at all, Bruce might never have stood forth and Bannockburn might never have been fought. It is for this that we honour him'.

Not lacking also is a fine tribute from a great English poet, William Wordsworth, 1770–1850. 'Wallace fought for Scotland and left the name of Wallace to be found like a wild flower all over his dear country.' Blind Harry, 1475, ends his *Life of Wallace*, 'Scotland he freed, brought it off bondage, and now in Heaven he has his heritage.' Another remarkable tribute also comes from an English source – after Wallace's execution, a saintly English hermit saw a vision of countless souls recently freed from purgatory standing aside freely and deferentially at the gates of Heaven, until the triumphant procession of Angels had carried the great patriot's soul into everlasting glory.

Monument to Wallace at Elderslie, near Paisley

The Wallace Monument, Stirling, was completed in 1869 as a memorial to the Scottish patriot

The Battle of Stirling Bridge

Bridge of Forth, bridge of worth,
Bridge for Scots to cross in peace,
Bridge of doom to aliens in birth,
Bridge for Scots a bridge of grace.

Roll on, o Forth, as once of yore,
You saw the Romans come and go.
Now gently bury the English dead,
'Tis Scotland's triumph, England's woe.

Great Wallace wisely looks ahead,
A battle won, but freedom not yet.
The path of peace and unity let's tread,
Till we our freedom in fullness get.

His death his foes thought 'twas his end.
Full freedom was for him not yet.
But freedom's torch the Bruce picked up,
And kept alight till Scots freedom get.

25 March 1984. 678th anniversary of Bruce's Coronation

Bruce to the Rescue

A summary of Bruce's activity up to 1306 is necessary to understand why and how he became King of Scots in that year. Born in 1274, probably at Turnberry, Ayrshire, one of Scotland's loveliest counties, Bruce, Earl of Carrick, was one of Scotland's greatest land-owners and magnates, and grandson of that Robert the Bruce, already mentioned as claiming by right of descent the Scottish throne in 1291. Bruce joined Wallace in 1297 in his fight for freedom, but he with others later that year capitulated and came back to allegiance to King Edward, at that time still trying to subjugate Scotland. It is not known why Bruce did this. Perhaps he was biding his time until the situation improved for him to help Wallace, for his submission meant he could keep his lands and even his life, and his delay in making his submission helped Wallace enormously.

In 1299 Bruce, John Comyn, and that outstanding patriot, Bishop William Lamberton of St Andrews, became Regents of Scotland. This remarkable bishop, whilst in Rome where he was consecrated bishop in June 1298, informed the Pope of the true state of affairs in Scotland. Consequently the Pope, Boniface VIII, wrote in 1298 to Edward urging him to release the Scots king, John Baliol, and to stop attacking Scotland. The next year Pope Boniface addressed a strongly worded letter 'Scimus fili' to Edward, condemning the English invasion of Scotland in the strongest terms, charging him with violation of Scottish national rights and stating: 'You yourself have to consider all this with due care'. It may be helpful to mention here the reasons behind this and other Papal interventions in England, Scotland and other countries during this time. All the Catholic countries of Europe regarded the Pope as the spiritual head of Christendom. As such, his duties included the defence of the international status quo and relations between kingdoms, both in peace and war. His position was like the present day United Nations condemning such things as apartheid or armed intervention in another country. Professor Barrow in his authoritative *Robert Bruce* points out that the Scots gained more support from that given them by Boniface VIII than what they had lost between 1305 and 1323 from the opposition of his successors. Since 1294 when Scotland was regarded by Edward of England as subject to him, the Popes had been consistently friendly to the Scots, as Barrow also points out.

About 1304 Bruce and Lamberton made a solemn bond of friendship and alliance. During the past nine years of the struggle against Edward, the bishop had made dangerous voyages which had exposed him to English privateers and capture. He had also engaged in strenuous diplomatic activity, knowing very well about all the lives lost at Berwick, Stirling Bridge, Falkirk and elsewhere, and the destruction of churches, villages, towns together with the miseries of hunger, famine and economic harm consequent on Scotland's rightful fight for freedom. So he was determined not to let all this 'blood, tears, toil and sweat', as Churchill said of Britain similarly fighting in World War II, to go for nothing.

Allied with him was another remarkable patriot, Robert Wishart, bishop of Glasgow, 1271–1316. And what about Bruce? The brutal killing of Wallace in 1305; the fact that Edward was now an ailing old man; the continuing importance of the community of the realm and his own strong claim to be King of Scots – all of this made him realise that the revival of kingship in Scotland was the only way by which Scotland once again could take its rightful and accustomed place among the free and independent nations of contemporary Europe. Perhaps personal ambition also spurred on his patriotism.

Bruce and John the Red Comyn of Badenoch were the two most powerful territorial magnates in Scotland. Comyn had been prominent in the long, arduous and costly struggle for Scotland's independence. Bruce fully realised that any plan to give Scotland a strong and free king would need the support of Comyn and all his family and fighting men if it was to succeed. So in February 1306, less than six months after Wallace's execution, the two men met by arrangement in the Franciscan Church in Dumfries. Apparently Bruce urged a revival of the Scottish kingship. What next happened, no one knows. Once before, in August 1299, Bruce and Comyn had quarrelled, Comyn seizing Bruce by the throat. Comyn seems to have neither approved nor supported Bruce's plan. Then it seems that the old antagonism burst out between these two high-spirited men and Bruce stabbed Comyn, who was either mortally injured or later killed by Bruce's followers.

Was Bruce's deed an act of self-defence? Was it a sudden fit of temper and deep resentment that Comyn would not join him in a further attempt to free Scotland? Did Comyn taunt Bruce for breaking faith to the English king? All this is unknown. Doubtless the deed was unpremeditated. It would be the act of a lunatic to act like this in a church and to incur the lasting enmity and animosity of perhaps the most influential family in Scotland. Bruce was a sober realist. Now he was the most powerful man in Scotland.

Did Bruce now decide to become King of Scots and win back his country's freedom? What he did seems to show that this was his decision, made perhaps as early as 1304, two years before. He swung into action and seized as many English-held castles as he could, for in those days of no artillery, those in castles were generally in control of the surrounding district. Baliol's kinsmen and supporters fled before him as also did the English, sheltering in safe castles or in England, which they should never have left, especially after the Pope's letter telling Edward to leave Scotland alone. Bruce was

Barra Castle, view from the south-east. This impressive building, rebuilt in 1614, stands near Oldmeldrum, Grampian. The King's Field to the south-east of the Castle was the site of Bruce's decisive victory over the Comyns. It is said that Bruce once slept here. Barra Castle now belongs to Mrs Quentin Irvine, who has done much to restore it.
Reproduced by courtesy of Edinburgh City Libraries

soon in Glasgow, about sixty miles north-west, conferring with that eminent patriot, Robert Wishart, its bishop. The bishop absolved Bruce from any sin, for Bruce, like any faithful Catholic, believed in the Church's power given her by Christ, her head, to forgive the repentant sinner his sins. King Edward, seemingly shocked at this, apparently persuaded the Pope to excommunicate Bruce. The Pope did so, as likely he did not know that Bruce had already been absolved by Bishop Wishart.

This excommunication was lifted in 1310, the Pope probably being better informed by now of what Bishop Wishart had done. This outstanding patriot did more than absolve Bruce. He preached that it was just as worthy to fight the English as to fight the heathen in the Holy Land. He brought out from hiding royal robes and a banner with the arms of the last rightful King of Scots, Alexander III, 1249–86. Bruce swore to guarantee the freedom of the Scottish Church, often harassed by claims of English supremacy. Already in 1192 the Pope declared the Scottish Church 'the special daughter of the Holy See'. So the Church was never again in serious danger of subordination to a foreign archbishop. The support of the Scottish Church and especially of bishops and higher clergy was very important for Bruce. The part played by the Scottish bishops all through the Scottish war of independence was crucial. Barrow's authoritative *Robert Bruce* makes this very clear. He states that the bishops and their officials 'were perhaps the biggest single obstacle to English pretensions north of the border'.

Crathes Castle, the ancestral home of the Burnetts of Leys. The Horn of Leys, on display in the Great Hall, is believed to be the original horn of tenure in virtue of which Robert Bruce granted the lands of Leys to Alexander Burnard in 1323

Robert the Bruce's Absolution 1306

I have to confess,
Dear Father in God,
I have deeply sinned,
May God spare me His rod.

The man and I
Were in Church in peace.
High words ensued,
He called me false.

My anger flamed out,
I struck him a blow
With dagger, alas,
And laid him low.

Appalled at the deed
I fled the Church,
My men rushed in,
Soon he was dead.

Ah, Father, forgive,
Sorrow fills me full.
And absolution now give,
As is Christ's rule.

Oh son, I forgive thee,
Through power Christ gave me.
And now I absolve thee,
From all sin I free thee.

For penance and welfare
Of that soul some slew
Betake to your care
Of his poor not a few.

Almsgiving like this
Gives glory to God,
Your punishment forgives
Spares you His rod.

So go in all peace, son,
Make the most of your life.
God in compassion
Gives him eternal life.

Father, I thank thee.
I'll do as you say.
Please pray I never,
An innocent slay.

Dear son, get crowned
King just and strong,
To fight Scotland's fight,
To right Scotland's wrong.

Scotland's Church is with you,
As she was with Saint Wallace.
So go now in God's grace,
And save our great Scots race. Amen.

23 August 1984. 679th anniversary of Wallace's death

Good King Robert's Coronation

'Blood, tears toil and sweat'
Are all I offer you just now.
This is our food and drink as yet,
Until our foes in submission bow.

Scotland's weal is ours to win,
And freedom from our foreign foe.
So let us this great task begin
And with God's help to battle go.

God wants His Scotland under none,
His dear Scots children in peace to live,
Not fearfully from foes to run,
But in His peace Him praise to give.

Our foe's sole claim is based on might,
To rule us by unjust command.
We take our stand on what is right –
The ancient freedoms of Scotland.

On to the work God wants us do,
His right hand helps, His Church's too.
These twain will always be with you,
If to them you're loyal and true.

And when our foes depart our land,
Compelled to go by our strong hand,
Then let us live for ever as one,
And we'll keep for ever all we've won.

May we our children our victory tell,
Their children hear from them our tale.
Let us for freedom strive always,
And never, never dear Scotland fail.

25 March 1984. 678th anniversary of Bruce's Coronation

Bruce's Coronation 1306

A centuries-old tradition for the coronation of the Kings of Scots is that the event takes place at Scone, near Perth. Robert the Bruce was fully aware of the great importance of the traditional rite. He was crowned on 25 March 1306 in the presence of Bishop Lamberton, Bishop Wishart, earls, nobility and clergy, and many other people. Bishop Lamberton of St Andrews performed the actual ceremony. Scotland once more had a king.

The Earl of Fife had the right of crowning the king and placing him on some substitute for the Stone of Destiny. (The real one was stolen by Edward and was until recently kept in Westminster Abbey, London, but has now been returned to Scotland.) The Earl was in Edward's power. So his twenty-year-old sister Isabel, wife of the Earl of Buchan, seized horses from her husband and rode off to Scone for the ceremony. Arriving too late, another ceremony took place on 27 March, Palm Sunday, when she placed the king on the throne and perhaps crowned him with a gold circlet.

Isabel's action is characteristic of those Scots women who through the ages have, like their menfolk, distinguished themselves by deeds of patriotism for their native country. The Bishop of St Andrews celebrated pontifical High Mass for the new king in connection with the placing of him on the throne. So now Bruce became Robert I, King of Scots, 1306, about two hundred and fifty years since the first king of most of Scotland, Malcolm III, 1057–93.

The new king acted promptly and vigorously. He probably issued a royal proclamation for all of goodwill, he seized more castles where possible, and began preparing for the great struggle he knew was imminent.

As for Edward, at first he could not believe that Bruce had acted like this. Then he faced this new and dangerous threat as forcefully as he could. His lieutenant was given full power 'to burn, slay and raise dragon', i.e. raise the dread dragon banner signifying that no mercy would be given and none of the acknowledged rights of war need be kept. Faithful Scots were caught and hanged. The great patriots, Bishop Lamberton and Bishop Wishart, were captured and sent to British prisons. Being bishops, they escaped hanging.

Bishop Wishart suffered all this until 1314 when he was released, going blind. He died two years after Bannockburn in peace in his own diocese of Glasgow, knowing that his dear Scotland was now free. He is one of our outstanding patriots, without whose help and encouragement Bruce might not have won through. Whenever I visualise his stately cathedral in Glasgow, I think of that gallant figure, his body now resting there in peace and helping on by his prayers in Heaven the descendants of those he helped so much on earth. His glorious memory lives on in Scottish hearts forever.

Left: *The Stone of Destiny was returned to Scotland in 1996. It is seen here with the 'Honours of Scotland'.*
Right: *Glasgow Cathedral – Bishop Wishart's final resting place*

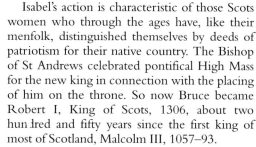

Goat Fell, Isle of Arran

Meanwhile Bruce's position was desperate. The English were amused and christened Bruce 'King Hob', i.e. 'King Bobby'. Bruce relied on his loyal followers, his courage, his great physical strength and his deep devotion to one of Scotland's most famous saints, Fillan of Glendochart. His queen and other royal and noble ladies, sent for safety to the north, were seized in the sanctuary of St Duthac in Tain, a gross violation of ecclesiastical and civil law. Bruce's wife and the indomitable Isabel who had made Bruce's coronation so memorable were imprisoned in specially built cages built onto a castle wall. So much for Edward's chivalry, sad to say.

In September 1306, six months after his coronation, Bruce slipped out of Scotland to Rathlin Island, a few miles off the north-east tip of Ireland. Here perhaps took place the famous story of the spider. Seeing a spider trying six times to swing its thread from one rafter to another and failing, Bruce said 'I too have been in six battles and have failed. If the spider tries again and succeeds, I too will try again'. The spider tried again and succeeded. So Bruce too made another attempt, succeeded and won through. Perhaps Bruce also visited some islands of the Outer Hebrides, such as Uist and Barra, and the castle, Eilean Donan on Loch Alsh, for its chief was fighting for Bruce at Bannockburn, seven years later.

During this highly dangerous time Bruce was supported by Angus Og MacDonald, chief of Islay and other territories, and a noble lady, rejoicing in the name of Christiana of the Isles, i.e. of Rum, Eigg, Uist, Barra, Gigha and mainland Knoydart and Moidart. Returning to Kintyre in Scotland in February 1307, and then to the Island of Arran, Bruce sent a spy to his own Earldom of Garrick to light a fire at night if all seemed well. The spy thought the English too strong but someone did light a fire. So Bruce and his men sailed the twenty or so miles and landed in Turnberry where he had been born about thirty-four years before.

Left: *Brodick Castle, from where Bruce launched his liberation of the mainland*
Following page: *Eilean Donan Castle, the picturesque island castle, linked to the shore by a causeway*

Linlithgow Palace, which has been a royal residence of some kind since the twelfth century

The Fight for Scotland's Freedom 1307-14

Now begins perhaps the greatest heroic exploit of recorded history. The English, secure in Scottish castles, held Scotland in an iron grip. Scotland lay as if in chains, and until the castles were taken, she remained enslaved. After his defeats and near-disasters, Bruce and his followers slowly broke these chains one by one. By speed and surprise, sagacity and audacity they captured all but five of these castles between 1307 and 1314. These five – Berwick, Bothwell, Stirling, Jedburgh and Dunbar surrendered or were captured after Bannockburn. Castles once captured were made useless, so as not to become again a threat to Scotland.

At the capture of Perth in January 1313, Bruce, himself wading through the ditch's icy water up to his neck and with his rope ladder fitted with grappling hooks on his back, was second to scale the wall. In September 1313 Linlithgow Castle fell when a Scots farmer, William Binnock, stopped his haywagon under the portcullis and cut the traces, so that it was immobilised. The ambushed Scots, hearing the shouted signal, rushed in and captured the castle. This farmer represented the common people of Scotland, the great anonymous mass fighting for freedom. Five months later in February 1314, the Scots under James Douglas (knighted on the eve of Bannockburn, 23 June 1314), black surcoats hiding their armour and creeping in the open like cattle, captured

Roxburgh. Three weeks later, another famous commander, Thomas Randolph, not to be outdone by Douglas, scaled with his men the steep and slippery north precipice of Edinburgh Castle, the precipice seen from Princes Street. They were led by another common man hero, William Francis, who used to climb down that way from the castle to visit his girlfriend in the town and then climb back again – rock climbing or death! All this was achieved by the fact that Bruce was an outstanding leader with an engaging personality and charm of manner. He never shirked danger and inspired his men with his own audacity. His biographer, Barbour, says, 'The most cowardly, stouter (braver) he made than a leopard'.

On 7 July 1307, Edward I died in sight of Scotland, still unconquered after more than ten years of warfare. His son and successor Edward II (1307–27), was neither soldier nor statesman and of this the Scots were well aware, and they used the respite given them to strengthen their growing freedom. In March 1309, Bruce's first Parliament affirmed his right to be king and offered its loyalty and support. There were expeditions to Ireland to buy seemingly 'black market' English arms, which would be paid for with protection money given him by the Northern English, demoralised by Scottish raids, and unprotected by the inactivity of Edward II.

One of the most striking views of the north precipice of Edinburgh Castle, from Princes Street

Bannockburn *by Sir W. Allan in the Wallace Monument, Stirling.*
Reproduced by courtesy of Stirling District Council

These four lines from Burns 'Caledonia' sum up Bannockburn's enduring result.

The daring invaders, they fled or they died.
Thus bold, independent, unconquered and free,
Her bright course of glory for ever shall run,
For brave Caledonia immortal must be.

The Battle of Bannockburn 1314

The hard pressed commander of strategic Stirling Castle had promised to surrender it to the Scots, if no English force relieved it before St John the Baptist's Feast, midsummer day, 24 June 1314. The English king and army could not ignore this. Edward marched up to near the castle with about 15,000 foot and archers and about 2,000 heavily armed knights on strong war horses. The Scots had about 5,500 foot and 500 light cavalry but no knights on war horses. On 23 June a body of English knights attempting to reach the castle were repulsed by Scots spearsmen in their mobile schiltrons, well trained by Bruce to fight like this. The English knights could not break up the schiltron with its twelve-foot-long spears bristling like hedgehog quills. This heartened the Scots greatly, and still

Above and left: *Stained-glass windows in the Wallace Monument, Stirling. Reproduced by courtesy of Stirling District Council*

more so, when an English knight, De Bohun, seeing Bruce on a small pony encouraging his men ahead of their line spurred on his war horse to attack him. Skilfully avoiding the deadly lance by a deft movement of his mount, and rising in his stirrups as De Bohun was thundering past, Bruce, with marvellous timing, cleft De Bohun's helmet and skull with his battle-axe which was broken by the impact. To his commanders' reproaches, Bruce with humour replied, 'There goes my good battle-axe'. That evening the English army was encamped in a strong position, both flanks protected by streams and marshy ground.

Stirling Castle, where the Scots spearsmen trained by Bruce repulsed an English onslaught

Early next morning – the feast of the Birth of St John the Baptist, 24 June, midsummer day, Mass was celebrated for the Scots, a tradition later maintained for Montrose's men, Bonnie Prince Charlie's men, and on many British battlefields. The Benedictine Abbot of Arbroath, one of Bruce's closest friends, blessed the Scots with the famous relic of St Columba, the Monymusk Reliquary, and Bruce exhorted his troops to conquer or die, so eloquently expressed in Robert Burns' heroic poem, 'Scots, Wha Hae'. Bruce had decided to attack, for as a great general he realised that the English, owing to the natural obstacles and perhaps owing to some previously constructed by the Scots, were unable to deploy their overwhelming numbers effectively. Seeing the Scots advance on that narrow front, about one thousand yards in all, the English knights rode charging against them. The Scots schiltrons stood firm, took the shock, resisted it and broke it. More knights surged forward, but the Scots spearsmen in their schiltrons again stood firm. A fierce fight took place, but as the Scots pressed on, the English knights became so packed together owing to the narrowness of the front, that they became a confused demoralised mass. Some Welsh archers brought up on their left flanks were dispersed by Bruce's light cavalry, a masterly use of inferior cavalry in a battle. The archers should have been used first, but the English king or his commanders thought they, with their heavily armed knights on their strong war-horses, would ride down the Scots spearsmen. It reminds one of the strategic victory of the Allies at Midway in 1942, overwhelming power laid low by overweening pride.

Then Bruce ordered up his own division of Highlanders and Islemen, for Scots from most parts of the country were serving under Bruce. Their furious and impetuous charge Bruce seems to have thought as of the highest importance. His words to them to charge: 'My hope is constant in thee', passed into the Clanranald motto and gave them the honour of fighting on the Right of the Line thereafter.

The English king was persuaded to flee, especially as what was thought to be a new Scots army was seen advancing, really the guardians of the baggage, perhaps armed with some weapons. He fled and the English rout began. Many were killed, some captured and Stirling Castle surrendered. The booty was so enormous that it was said: 'Scotland became rich in a day'. It was total victory, Scotland's greatest victory, won by perhaps Scotland's greatest hero, ably supported by his loyal and devoted men firmly resolved to conquer or to die. It was perhaps Scotland's finest hour.

Bruce and his men by their total victory at Bannockburn had won the independence of Scotland. Bannockburn made Scots realise they were one people, one nation. Here we come to adult nationhood. Before the battle the Scots prayed, as they were to do on many a battlefield in many lands. Edward II seeing them, said: 'See, they are asking for mercy'. 'True', was the answer, 'but not from you. Those men will win or perish'.

Win they did, and we today realise more than ever what it meant for Scots. The 700th anniversary of Bannockburn will be with us in less than thirty years. Under God's providential care, we see how often He preserved Bruce and our other leaders with him from defeats, disasters and sudden deaths. So this continuing Divine care enabled the foundations Bruce and others laid to be a secure base on which Scotland's later achievements, both for herself and for the world, could be erected. In religion, culture, literature, science and other fields Scots have offered and offer much. The Hall of Heroes in the Wallace Monument already mentioned gives us a galaxy of famous Scots. But since its completion in 1869, new stars have appeared in our galaxy, such as J. L. Baird, television pioneer, Sir R. Watson-Watt, pioneer of British radar, so decisive in the Battle for Britain in World War Two, and Earl Haig, pioneer of ex-servicemen's associations. The freedom won by Bannockburn helped greatly to accomplish all of this. Bruce and his collaborators, clerical and lay, built better than they knew.

Robert Burns seems to sum it up best when in 1793 he wrote his immortal lines of Bruce's address to his troops before Bannockburn:

> Scots, wha hae (who have) wi' Wallace bled,
> Scots, wham (whom) Bruce has aften led,
> Welcome to your gory bed,
>   Or to victorie!

The next year, 1794, Burns again put all of our thoughts into the following memorable words: 'Independently of my enthusiasm as a Scotsman, I have rarely met with anything in history which interests me as a man equal with the story of Bannockburn. A cruel but able usurper leads the finest army in Europe to extinguish the last spark of freedom among a great-daring, greatly injured people. Against this, the desperate remnants of a gallant nation devote themselves to rescue their bleeding country or perish with her. Liberty! Thou art a prize truly and indeed invaluable, for never canst thou be too dearly bought.'

Blind Harry's concluding words about Wallace fittingly apply also to Bruce:

> Scotland he freed, brought it off bondage.
> And now in Heaven he has his heritage.

Right: *Loch Trool, Dumfries and Galloway. The Bruce Stone, which commemorates Bruce's victory over the English in 1307, stands at the south-western end*

Good King Robert 1314~29

Bruce was now indeed King of Scots; clergy, nobles and ordinary Scots, for the most part, resolutely and enthusiastically with him. To overcome mighty England, to defeat her so overwhelmingly at Bannockburn and to restore the venerable Scots monarchy were certainly outstanding achievements. But still greater achievements are to be recorded of this remarkable warrior and statesman king.

Edward II and his successor, Edward III (1327–77), would not admit that Scotland was an independent kingdom. So Bruce resorted to invasions of England to force them to make peace and admit Scotland's independence. Now the Pope, not knowing the true state of affairs, very likely due to English 'reports', and appreciating the now internationally well-known fighting qualities of Bruce and his men wanted them and the English to join in a crusade against the Turks. To envoys from two cardinals proposing the Pope's terms for peace, Bruce kindly and humorously replied that he could not open the Pope's letter addressed to 'Robert Bruce', as there were several men so

called, and he would not open the Pope's sealed letters, for they carried no royal title. This and other matters involving Bruce's recognition as king led to the Pope excommunicating the king. To students of this period this does not mean much, especially when, as then in Scotland, all the bishops of the Scots were in support of Bruce. They and the well-educated clergy, who had studied and were well-known at leading universities such as Paris, Cologne, and Bologna, knew that a papal excommunication was null and void, if its reasoning was, as here, unsound.

In 1319 the Pope summoned four leading Scots bishops to Rome. To help the Pope realise the true state of affairs, the chief men in Scotland, all laymen, but obviously with the king and bishops breathing down their necks, drew up the outstanding Declaration of Arbroath, 6 April 1320, a landmark in constitutional law and history, not only for Scotland but also for other kingdoms. It was and is a most remarkable letter, and judging from the copy still preserved, it was beautifully written and sealed with the seals of the signers, a masterpiece of terse yet rhythmic Latin, a

Melrose Abbey, founded by David I in 1136

masterly exposition of Scots history as then understood and based partly on Pope Boniface's stern letter to Edward I in 1299, and of the relations of the King to the community of the realm. Those signing stated: 'Through the grace of Him who wounds and heals, we have been freed from so many great evils by the bravery of our Lord and Sovereign Robert. The Providence of God, his deserts, the lawful succession and our common and just consent have all made him our king. If he yields to England – this with a very knowing smile – we would cast him out and choose another king. So long as only one hundred of us are left, we

will never yield to England's domination. We fight not for glory, not for wealth, not for honour. We fight for freedom which no good man surrenders but with his life.' No finer statement of a claim to national independence was produced anywhere in contemporary Europe. It is perhaps the highest mark of and tribute to

the learning and culture of contemporary Scotland, a Scotland nearly ruined by more than twenty years of war, despoliation, starvation, imprisonments and executions.

The Scots were leaving nothing to chance. Two of the Scots nobility carried the Declaration of Arbroath to the Pope along seemingly with letters from Bruce and Bishop Lamberton mentioning papal privileges to Scotland, and perhaps a copy of the letter of Pope Boniface to Edward I which asked him to leave Scotland alone. Unfortunately, we do not know how the Pope received the letter. Certainly he could take no offence. The Scots were writing as any good Catholic would, full of respect for the Pope and for what they held him to be, the spiritual head of Christendom, with a right to call errant sons to repent when they transgressed international law. It must have opened his eyes about the real state of affairs between England and Scotland and helped to justify Bruce and his actions. It must also have opened his eyes in other ways too. Could such a well-drawn up letter, written in such clear and concise Latin, perhaps even better than his own, be the work of ignorant scoundrels? Doubtless too he questioned the two Scots nobles and others present about Scotland's recent fight for independence and perhaps he knew about the letter mentioned above of his predecessor, Boniface, for papal policy tries to be consistent with past policy. In 1323 the Earl of Moray put clearly before the Pope the reasons why he should recognise Bruce as king. Perhaps this was the deciding factor, for in January next year, 1324, the Pope decided to address Bruce as king.

Doubtless Edward II heard of all this and in 1324 he sent a strong mission to Rome, asking that no one in Scotland should be made a Scottish bishop, 'for it is the prelates (bishops) of Scotland who encourage the nobility, gentry and people in their evil acts'. A neutral observer knowing how the support of the clergy was crucial for Scotland's independence, might comment: 'Good for them'. The Pope in his reply to this outrageous demand shows him acting as the responsible head of Christendom. Although Bruce was still excommunicated, the Pope replied that since no Englishman could enter Scotland, the people would have no bishops, something he could not allow. Perhaps

Dunfermline Abbey, where Bruce is buried in the choir, his grave marked by a modern brass

too the efforts of the Scots in Rome and Edward's effrontery made him still more aware of the true state of affairs in Scotland.

In 1315 Edward, Bruce's only surviving brother (two had been hanged by the English, the third had died), led an expedition to Ireland to accept the crown of 'free' Ireland offered him by the King of Tyrone and others. Bruce joined him in 1316. Perhaps Bruce meant by this expedition to use Ireland as a base to attack England. But it was a diversion of men and resources he could not afford and it all came to nothing when Edward was killed in Ireland in 1318.

At last the new English king, Edward III (1327–77), realised Bruce would have to be acknowledged as king of an independent Scotland. On 17 March 1328, the treaty of Edinburgh gave Scotland full freedom, and by it King Edward solemnly renounced all claims to sovereignty over Scotland. The English king, to his credit, promised to do all he could to have Bruce and his bishops freed from the papal excommunication. This was done by the Pope in October of this same great year for the Scots. It also seems to show that English machinations were responsible for the original imposition of this excommunication. However, the Scots were glad to be once more in full communion with the rest of Christendom.

Ever since Bannockburn, Bruce had been rebuilding the shattered economy, passing wise measures in Parliament, pardoning his enemies when he could, and for his dead relatives and friends enabling Mass to be offered 'for the repose of their souls', something every faithful Catholic does or, after death, wants done for him. No wonder he fully merited the rare honour of being called 'Good King Robert'. His deep and strong religious faith comes out most clearly according to Barrow in his authoritative *Robert Bruce* in the painful and slow pilgrimage which the now ailing Bruce made to the famous shrine of St Ninian at Whithorn in Galloway in April 1329, hardly more than two months before he died. In this connection it is pleasing to record that this custom of going on pilgrimage is now being revived, and that the annual ecumenical pilgrimage to Ladykirk and St Mary's Church, Haddington, is very beneficial to many participants. This pilgrimage also clearly proves that Bruce was no leper, as no attempt was made to segregate the king, as was the very strict law for all lepers – including kings.

Then the time for his reward came for our heroic and 'Good' king on 7 June 1329. Again there is a most remarkable tribute to his sterling Christian spirit. Addressing the nobles and others present at his death-bed, he declared: 'After my death, I want my heart to be taken from my body and to go to the Holy Sepulchre of Christ in Jerusalem. I had made a solemn vow when things were at their worst for me, to go on the Crusades after I had obtained peace for this realm'. Surely a most remarkable instance of outstanding Christian love and devotion to Christ. Bearing Bruce's heart in a casket, Sir James Douglas 'the Good', while fighting against the Moors in Spain was, with his companions, overcome and slain. The heart of Bruce and the body of Douglas were brought back to Scotland. The heart was buried in Melrose Abbey, which Bruce had loved so well, and Douglas was buried in the parish church of Douglas, about ten miles from Lanark.

The body of the great king, perhaps Scotland's greatest, was buried in Dunfermline Abbey beside the shrine of his gracious ancestress, St Margaret, wife and queen of King Malcolm Canmore, 1058–93.

What a stirring example of fortitude in adversity the life and exploits of King Robert the Bruce are for us in Scotland today. They are a constant inspiration for us, as they have been to many in the past, such as Robert Burns and Sir Walter Scott, to act resolutely and with fortitude in adversity, and to make ever more real the vision of a free Scotland which sustained Bruce and his collaborators during those more than twenty years of so arduous a struggle, till they gained Scotland's full freedom for ever from foreign foes. What a man to be admired. What a Scot to be emulated. What a Christian to be imitated.

Bruce and the Spider. Reproduced by courtesy of the Mitchell Library, Glasgow

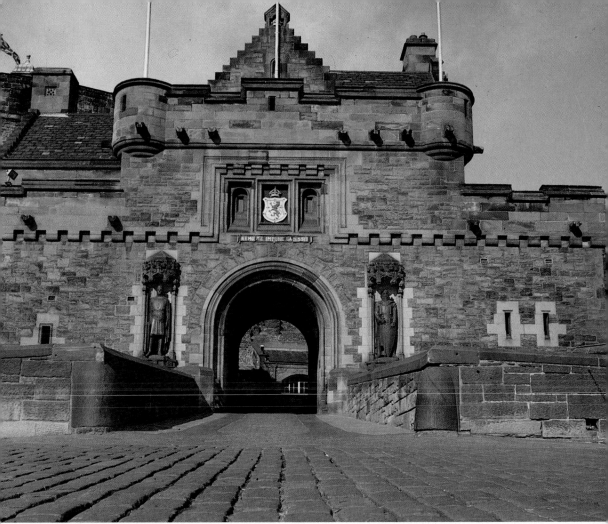

The statues of Wallace (right) and Bruce (left) either side of the archway at Edinburgh Castle. Reproduced by courtesy of Historic Buildings and Monuments, Scotland

Robert the Bruce's Dying Prayer

Good King Robert is near to death,
That great heart is beating so slow,
Around his bed in tears all stand,
Dreading and fearing he has to go.

Good King Robert with trembling voice:
'No need to weep, no need of tears.
My life is aye in Christ's saving hands,
About me and Scotland have no fears.

You'll have no fear, if united you stay,
All foes will break on unity's rock.
Be just and kind and strong and brave,
And at your foes you'll always mock.

Good King Robert puts hand on heart,
'This heart aye beat for God and Scotland.
When things were blackest, I vowed to go,
And fight for God against His foe.

My vow, alas, I could not keep,
For care of Scotland drove me full hard.
But now when body in death doth sleep,
My heart must go where Christ made peace.'

'We'll do, good King, all that you've said,
And lay your heart where Christ made peace.'
Thankful and tearful the great king prayed,
'Now dismiss Thy servant, O Lord, in Peace.
                              Amen.'

7 June 1984. 655th anniversary of Good King Robert's death

Scots Wha Hae

'There is a tradition' says Burns in a letter to Thomson, 'that the old air "Hey, Tuttie Taitie" was Robert Bruce's March at the Battle of Bannockburn. This thought in my solitary wanderings has warmed me to a pitch of enthusiasm, on the theme of liberty and independence which I have thrown into a kind of Scottish ode fitted to the air that one might suppose to be the gallant Scot's address to his heroic followers on that eventful morning.'

Scots, wha hae wi' Wallace bled,
Scots, wham Bruce has aften led,
Welcome to your gory bed,
   Or to victorie!

Now's the day, and now's the hour:
See the front o' battle lour,
See approach proud Edward's power —
   Chains and slaverie!

Wha will be a traitor knave?
Wha can fill a coward's grave?
Wha sae base as be a slave? —
   Let him turn, and flee!

Wha for Scotland's King and Law
Freedom's sword will strongly draw,
Freeman stand or freeman fa',
   Let him follow me!

By Oppression's woes and pains,
By your sons in servile chains,
We will drain our dearest veins
   But they shall be free!

Lay the proud usurpers low!
Tyrants fall in every foe!
Liberty's in every blow!
   Let us do, or die!

Robert Burns, 1759–96